WAKEY, WAKEY

WAKEY, WAKEY

Will Eno

THEATRE COMMUNICATIONS GROUP
NEW YORK
2019

Wakey, Wakey is published by Theatre Communications Group,
Inc., 520 Eighth Avenue, 24th Floor, New York, NY 10018-4156

Wakey, Wakey is published by arrangement with Oberon Books,
Ltd. 521 Caledonia Road, London, N7 9RH

The publication of *Wakey, Wakey* by Will Eno, through TCG's
Book Program, is made possible in part by the New York State
Council on the Arts with support of Governor Andrew Cuomo
and the New York State Legislature.

TCG books are exclusively distributed to the book trade by
Consortium Book Sales and Distribution.

A catalogue record for this book is available from the Library of
Congress

ISBN 978-1-55936-578-9 (trade paper)
ISBN 978-1-55936-893-3 (ebook)

Cover image by Joyce O'Connor/Radiant1
First TCG Edition, February 2019

In regular and loving memory of
Ada Louise Huxtable, Jim Houghton, and Edward Albee

CHARACTERS

GUY

*male, 40s-60s, youthful looking but might suddenly
look gaunt or unwell, in the wrong (right) lighting.*

LISA

*female, late 30s-50s. A warm and caring person,
but not inclined toward any kind of sentimentality.
Loving, and, matter-of-fact, in equal amounts.*

There are some additional production notes at
the end of the play.

STAGE SETTING

*mainly empty except for a number of taped-up moving boxes, and a
small pile of clothes. Other signs of someone packing up and moving.
A wall with wainscoting or a chair rail, some specific-enough detail
to suggest a particular room – maybe the common room of a hospital
(probably a building from the early 1900s up to the 1950s or so).
A practical electrical outlet in the wall and a dimmer switch, both in
the ordinary places. A phone charger is plugged into the outlet.
A doorway, somewhere off to the side and back, either practical or
a free-standing theatrical door, perhaps with plants or small shrubs
on either side of it. A calendar with all the actual days up to today's
performance date X-ed out. The calendar is hung low enough so that
someone in a wheelchair could write in it. Some other ordinary things
may appear in the set.*

Wakey, Wakey received its world premiere on February 27, 2017 at Signature Theatre (Paige Evans, Artistic Director; Erika Mallin, Executive Director; Jim Houghton, Founder) in New York City. It was directed by Will Eno, the set design was by Christine Jones, the costume design was by Michael Krass, the lighting design was by David Lander, the sound design was by Nevin Steinberg, the projections design was by Peter Nigrini; the production stage manager was David H. Lurie. The cast was:

GUY	Michael Emerson
LISA	January LaVoy

HOUSE LIGHTS GO SLOWLY TO HALF, AND THEN FADE OUT TO BLACK.

HARD LIGHTS UP. Perhaps LED light, so there's no fade up or down. GUY is lying face-down on the stage in pajama pants, pulled up to his knees, with no shirt. After a moment, he lifts his head.

GUY: Is it now? I thought I had more time.

HARD LIGHTS OUT.

SOUND: *MUZAC plays, as in a "technical difficulties" moment. The initial production used "Spanish Flea" by Herb Alpert.*

After a few moments, maybe 2 or 3 seconds:

PROJECTION: *A projection that reads "No Applause" blinks on the back wall. As quickly as possible, music drops out,*

HARD LIGHTS BACK UP, and we see GUY, dressed in a suit jacket, a dress shirt, no tie, and pajama pants. He is sitting in a wheelchair and wearing slippers or comfortable shoes.

GUY: *(Quietly, to himself.)* Wow, that was quick. *(To AUDIENCE.)* This was, what's the best way to say it, this was supposed to be something else. This was going to be a whole different thing.

Very brief pause.

1

But, you know, tick tock, tick tock. *(Brief pause.)*
That's the sound of a clock, for you youngsters.

I see some familiar faces, out there. Or, to be
honest, I see some recognizable shapes. *(Very
brief pause.)* I don't see those things, to be
honest. I hope you're there, I think you are.

I'm starting to adjust a little, here. The iris, or
whatever part that is, is, you know, starting to
adjust. Hello, world.

*He points at someone in the audience. As if he's saying,
in a very low-key way, "Hey, I know this guy." A sort of
eerie moment, as he continues pointing, for too long. He
then slowly stops, and looks away for a moment, without
a discernible expression. Brief pause.*

Sorry, that came off as sort of menacing. I just
meant it as a reminder. A friendly reminder
that, what? A reminder that some day,
perhaps, when you least expect it, someone in
a theater is going to point at you. Hi.

He looks at the boxes and around the stage.

Cardboard boxes. This is all from before.
There's always this whole other world, isn't
there. Desk drawers full of notes and sketches.
The secret plans and ideas of people who time
ran out on. Over a hundred thousand people
died today. When we try to think about that,
we probably forget that a hundred thousand

people died yesterday. And a hundred thousand the day before that. There are a hundred thousand people who've been dead for three days. The coffee cakes and casseroles from friends are slowly disappearing; the families and loved ones, heading back to work, returning the odd phone call. People are plodding along, in the face of such total… Oh, but we're not here to mope, right? We're here to listen to music and drink some grape juice, maybe get a free T-shirt. We're here to say good-bye, of course – there's always someone or something to say good-bye to, and it's important to honor the people whose shoulders we stood upon and fell asleep against. So, yes, we're here to say good-bye and maybe hopefully also get better at saying hello. To celebrate Life, if that doesn't sound too passive-aggressive. *(Very brief pause.)* Or, I don't know, what do I know – I was asleep in my PJ's five minutes ago. Three minutes, 55 seconds, to be exact *(NOTE: or whatever this time actually is)*. Sorry, I don't know exactly what to say to you. *(Very brief pause.)* I wonder how you hear that, how that strikes you? What do you make of the fact that this event, painstakingly scripted, rehearsed, designed, and directed, features someone saying, "I don't know exactly what to say to you." *(Brief pause.)* I hope you'll receive that in the humble and hopeful spirit it was offered in. I know, I know – Intentions. Them and a cup of coffee won't get you five cents at the zoo, or however that goes.

Whatever the reality, I hope we can agree
that: here we are. People talk about matters of
Life and Death. But it's really just Life, isn't it?
When you think about it?

Brief pause.

A joke would be good, right around here. *(To
himself.)* A joke would be so funny right now.

Brief pause.

SOUND: *A very distant siren that seems to pass outside the
theater.*

GUY: Oh my God, perfect – did you hear? The
siren? Did you just… *(Very brief pause.)* I guess
it's gone. Was it a police car or an ambulance?
You know? They're coming for you, but what
are they coming to do? It's all coming, and at
very high speed, but is it good news or bad? If
you don't know the answer, I won't ruin it for
you.

But so what are we here for? I don't mean
that in the big way. Just, you know, right
here. You're going to be in this room for a
little over three hours – what do you want to
have happen? What do you want to feel? Joy?
Relief? A sense that those who are gone have
been honored and made present? A sense that
those who are here have been given strength
for the journey ahead? If you just think of this
as a dry place to eat while you plan your next

4

move, or somewhere where you might find a pen on the floor, you probably won't be too disappointed. However you think of it, right now, is probably how you'll think of it when it's over. And, whoever you are, you know, out in the lobby or commuting to work, that's who you'll be on your deathbed. So, push yourself, a little. And, go easy on yourself, a little. Time is your friend and time is your enemy. We can choose which, for a while. This isn't three hours, by the way. It probably won't even be one. I just said that to make life more exciting. Now you've suddenly got two free hours to do whatever you want with. Hooray! Call up the grandkids. Have sex with the wrong person. Just… enjoy. *(Brief pause.)* This was originally going to be something else. I don't know what it is, now. Maybe it's something called "Elegy for the Eulogist," or something sad and circular with a lot of l's and g's in it like that.

Anyway, let's proceed. You should all have some 3D glasses in a pouch on the side of your seat. *(Brief pause.)* That's another joke. If there's a pouch on the side of your seat, I don't know what it is and I certainly wouldn't put your hand in there.

(Very brief pause. Referring to himself being seen in some kind of 3D technology.) Can you imagine? The, you know… *(In a very small gesture, he mimes putting on some glasses.)*

He waves his arms around a little, as if he's being seen in 3D. Movements that look as if he's underwater, or in slow-motion, for example. This could be slightly beautiful and eerie, for a second.

"Whoa! It's almost like he's right here in the room with us."

He continues with the movement, for a few seconds more. Maybe one particular movement, toward the end of the above line, causes him some pain. Brief pause.

Did I seem real?

He reaches to rub his back.

Ooh, I think I did something funny. Not "Funny – ha-ha," but more "Funny – I injured my back." Sorry.

He rings the bell that's attached to the wheelchair.

(Toward backstage.) Hello? *(Brief pause. Explaining the bell.)* This is good for when the throat gets dry.

But why don't we keep going.

He takes some index cards (20 or 30), held together with a rubber band, out of the pocket on the wheelchair. Looks at the card that's on the top of the stack.

I probably don't need these. They're sort of a crutch, but…. *(He reads.)* "Try to create

a respectful mood, but one in which there
is joy and light." Oops. I don't know if I've
been doing that. Although, actually, I just
remembered – we have some music for this,
for setting that particular mood.

*He very subtly signals to the booth, and then sits waiting.
No music seems to play at first but then,*

SOUND: *a subliminal sound design (perhaps distant real-
world sounds, subtly treated and arranged) begins
to play, developing into a ghost of music, something
that in some Universe might be suited to setting
a mood of respectfulness, joy, and light. There is
something subtly beautiful about it. He listens, takes
a peek at an index card, looks up at the booth with
a sort of skeptical look. The "music," having only
played for ten or fifteen seconds, ends.*

GUY: I'm not sure if – I don't know if that was it. We
have a lot of people pitching in here, so, not
sure. Maybe that was it. If so, Bravo. A totally
quiet song. Maybe it had a really grand title
like "Joy and Light." Maybe those were the
themes, of the song we didn't hear. A world-
famous psychologist I know, who's actually
an exterminator and a huge Miami Dolphins
fan, believes that certain words can carry their
meaning right into our bodies. That hearing
certain words can create the realities behind
those words, in the hearer, in the hearer's
body. Joy, Light. *(Very quietly.)* Happiness?
Clarity? Patience. Your favorite meal. Your

favorite sweater. Calm. *(Brief pause.)* Anything?
It probably takes a little while.

Brief pause.

But not to fear. Plenty of stuff on the program.
(Mostly to himself.) Now where is that…

*He feels around underneath him in the wheelchair, looking
for something, and looks around the stage.*

(Still to himself.) Did I leave it back – no, there
it is.

*There's a remote control device sitting on a box, ten feet
away, out of sight of the audience. With a little bit of
difficulty, he gets up from his wheelchair and moves toward
the remote. He takes a few steps.*

(Triumphantly.) I can walk! *(He picks up the
remote, begins to return to his wheelchair.)* I mean,
I could before, but still. Pretty amazing. *(He
sits.)* But to be serious, there actually was a
time I couldn't walk. *(He clicks the remote.)*

PROJECTION: *Baby picture, a photo of a smiling six-
month-old boy lying on his tummy (baby picture of
the actor).*

That really takes me back. Wow. That's a while
ago. Look at the hair style. *(To the booth.)* Could
we have that music back again?

SOUND: *Perhaps it's a slight enrichment of the "music" cue we heard earlier. He is quietly moved and pleased, as he looks up at the baby picture.*

He clicks the remote control.

PROJECTION: *Another photo of the actor as a toddler. He clicks, and another photo, perhaps a wider shot of many children. He clicks again, and it's a photo of a girl of two or three, eating ice cream. There is ice cream all over her face.*

GUY: Ice cream. *(He reads another index card.)* This is, some of these are sort of incomplete, they're not even, well, I'll just read it. "Maybe a part about Mortality. Genes. Something about Anxiety or the Big Secret we all share. Something about the Eyes." I don't remember what this is. Some idea, I guess. Some big idea. I had capitalized certain words. Honestly don't remember. *(He looks up at the picture of the girl eating ice cream.)* Hmmm. Well, sorry. *(Brief pause. Looks off to the side.)* I remember, when I was really little, some holiday, and there was a punch bowl, and – *(Still distracted by what he had intended with the index card, he looks up at the photo again.)* you know what, maybe it was just to just look and think. And see whatever you see. Maybe that was the idea. Is – and I don't know – is there something in the eyes that, no matter what the momentary expression, is always there and everyone can see? Dread? Courage. Knowledge? Fear of the unknown? Calmness in the face of the known? I guess that was the question – is there something recognizably human, something that's always the same, in everybody's eyes? *(Looking at the picture again.)* Poor kid – all these big words getting hung around her neck. She'll be okay. There's definitely something there. I think so, anyway. Something light and real and lasting. Until it's gone, I guess.

Brief pause. He's staring at the next card.

This, um… well, here: *(He reads.)* "The truest kind of courage is barely noticeable, until you look back someday in a noticing mood." *(Very brief pause.)* I remember exactly what I was talking about, with this one. That sort of plain but unbelievable courage some people have. At the time, when you're around it, it just seems like kindness, even happiness, like a little kid eating ice cream. It's very quiet, true bravery. It's a person on a Friday afternoon, nauseous and afraid, saying "hi." Saying, "Sit down right here. Move that cushion." Like my friend Joanne's mother before her spinal surgery. Or, Joanne. And others, of course. All kinds of others. *(Referring to toddler photo.)* Okay, get your last looks in. Say "bye-bye."

Clicks remote, photo disappears. Clicks again, a "blank" slide appears; clicks again, and another blank. And then:

PROJECTION: *A photo of some people sitting at a nondescript institutional-looking cafe.*

GUY: I don't know what this is doing in here. *(Looks out to audience.)* Probably just a stock image we got, to fill up some time. *(Brief pause.)* Nope. It's the patients-only cafeteria in the End-of-Life-Care wing of Creighton DuPont Memorial Hospital. Should've just had that written right on the slide, so there wouldn't be any confusion.

Quickly and fairly flatly, but with some care, to audience member:

How you doing? Okay?

Continuing on, while looking through the index cards.

It's funny how sometimes you think you know what you're looking at and then, surprise surprise, you turn out to be right.

He looks through some more cards.

(To himself, as he checks through the cards.) Did that, did that. That doesn't actually exist. And we can skip this, too, I think. *(Comes to the right card.)* Ah, right – of course. *(Tucks cards underneath him, on wheelchair seat.)*

I hope everyone has a favorite teacher or an important person somewhere in their past. Maybe a grandparent, a boss, anyone, even your kids, a son or daughter. Someone way back who nudged you a couple of degrees in this direction or that, and now, after all that time and distance, the whole trajectory of your life, because of that tiny change, is unrecognizably different. A little nudge, a hug, and we slowly, quietly change, and for the rest of our life our new different life is partly a tribute to this other person, it's even an expression of this other person. Immortality? Nudge, nudge. *(Brief pause.)* Anyway, I hope we can take a private second just to think of that person, to wish them courage wherever they're going, or peace if they've already gone. And to help that along, we have a – some of you have probably seen the YouTube video on this, the, um, the grandfather on the Ferris Wheel? – we have a special audio tone that's supposed to support feelings of gratitude. I know, it sounds crazy and it's probably not real. But, it apparently kind of activates and even sort of massages something called the anterior cingulate cortex, which is right here *(Points to crown of his head.)* And which is where we experience thanks, possibly. They say practicing gratitude can physically change the shape of the brain. In a good way. But, so, okay: someone who loved or encouraged you. Couple good breaths, then, here we go: Give private thanks. If you want. The tone is going to start in just a couple – *(Tone begins.)*

SOUND: *Maybe something like a shofar or a simple horn quietly and gently begins. It slowly shifts in sound and tone. It should be unique. Perhaps at some point GUY turns to look at the slide of the Hospice cafeteria, which is still being projected against the wall. The sound plays for 15 or 20 seconds total, maybe with a dense and complicated part in the middle with a screaming human voice buried deep down in it, and then gently fades. Brief pause.*

GUY: Great. Thank you. Hmm. Don't know about the special tone – the jury's still out on that, but, I don't think it hurt. Some of you, maybe, some of you were getting waves of thanks while you were thanking someone else. Nice to think of all that stuff flowing around. Which it probably always is, but it's, yeah, maybe the sound helped take it to a higher level.

And on that note, we have a very special guest joining us tonight. I'm sure you were all expecting something like this so, without further ado, because I know our guest needs no introduction.

He stares calmly at the audience, perhaps bites at a cuticle and then continues on, easily, and entirely as if there had been no interruption and no Special Guest announced.

We were talking about time, earlier. The idea of it, the feel of it. Friend, enemy, co-conspirator, I'm sure you have your own relation. Maybe you say, "Time took my Dad. I hate Time. Time took away my sister." I don't know if you say that. If you do, I'm sorry, and,… I'm sorry. I'm not going to, I'm not going to try to argue and say, "But Time gave us your Dad. Time gave us your sister. Let's raise a glass to Time." No. I know. Certain feelings are not to be answered with thoughts. *(He turns and clicks off the slide of the hospice cafeteria. Very gently.)* I'm sure what you're feeling is right. Maybe it's sad, maybe it's gratitude, or being angry – there's room. You, you know, you had a wish, a different idea, but, another reality arrived, or a particular illusion ended, and, here we are, making do, and you have every right to feel as… you know. I wish there was something, um, I wish I could help. *(Very brief pause. He whispers, trying to get the reality into our bodies.)* Joy. Light. *(A little more regularly.)* My condolences. *(He clears his throat. Regular voice.)* This might be totally the wrong direction, but, maybe we can look at this…

He clicks remote. The house lights blink up for a second.

Nope. Sorry. *(He clicks again, house lights down. He keeps working with the remote.)* These guys set this up for me, so that I could kind of manage all the different – here we are.

PROJECTION: *A menu comes up, projected on the wall. He clicks through menu options to "play video."*

GUY: *(Quietly.)* This is… um, let me make sure I'm doing this right. HDMI, component 1, and then it should – yes. *(Video gray appears on back wall.)* Um, about the thing itself… Pretty self-explanatory. *(Video plays, with very short lead-in, on back wall.)*

PROJECTION: VIDEO: *a video montage of animals screaming. GUY turns upstage to watch. It's all*

*animals, except for one brief clip of Luciano
Pavarotti singing a high note, somewhere towards
the end. Lights adjust. The video is maybe 40
seconds to a minute long. It's a fun diversion, offered
in lightness.* GUY *stays still, facing away from the
audience. Maybe we see him shaking, just a little bit,
and it's unclear whether he is laughing or crying. He
returns to the audience, looking fairly serious.*

GUY: Animals. *(Brief pause.)* I hope that was, you
know, enjoyable. At least a little. If you were
enjoying yourself – I get a big kick out of
that sort of stuff for some reason – but if you
enjoyed that silly thing 30 seconds ago, where
does that go, if anywhere? The enjoyment.
Bones, cells, nowhere? *(Brief pause.)* I'm not
trying to sound smart, here. To which I'm sure
you would say, "Yeah, that's not – I would not
worry about that. Not a big risk." *(Very brief
pause.)* I hope it lingers, is all. I hope it sticks to
the ribs, somehow.

But, so, if our lives can be divided up at all,
then can't they be divided up into two parts,
the part before and the part after we watched a
video of screaming animals? If so, and I think
it's so, welcome to the second part of your life.
Wow. Here we really are. You made it. How's it
feel? I wonder what you'll do. No turning back
now. I think you're going to be amazing. *(Very
brief pause.)* Why not. Why not.

By the way, did everyone get a release form to
sign? You shouldn't have. There's no release

form. See, just more and more good news. No
release forms are necessary. Nothing is being
asked of you here. Legally.

SOUND: *Very distant squealing truck brakes, outside the theater.*

GUY: Oh, I like that. Sounded like a medieval
instrument. *(Another brief little sound.)* What was it?

As he's looking through his cards.

A truck or something? Truck brakes.

*Still looking through cards. A phrase occurs to him that
happily marries the outside-the-theater and inside-the-
theater worlds:*

Somebody trying to deliver something.

Okay, let's look at this and see if there's anything
interesting about it. *(He clicks the remote.)*

PROJECTION: *Some kind of optical illusion or a design that
is momentarily confusing to look at.*

*GUY stares at the image for a moment and then takes a
sandwich out of the pocket on his wheelchair. He makes a
cautious attempt at eating it, but can't, and puts it away.*

GUY: Ugghhh. I can't eat this. *(Very brief pause.)* I
shouldn't be eating anyway, that's rude. But,
the body's always there, like a little child. I
just remembered *(Pointing to image projection)*
– maybe this thing reminded me. Oh, I

should turn it off *(He clicks the remote, the image disappears.)*, so it doesn't melt your brain or whatever it's doing – but I was waiting for a train, once. A while ago. I guess it was rush hour or a holiday and, but, everyone was looking sideways towards the tunnel, watching for the coming train. This is a very little story, but I'm trying to remember it exactly because even though it was so normal it was also somehow, like, blessed or something. Blessèd. There was that muffled noise, the distant little clank you hear, the creaking of the rails. There was a little light way down the tunnel and little pieces of paper started floating along on the tracks, and the sound of the train got louder, while everyone stared into the tunnel, all just very everyday. People looked scared. People looked happy, tired, curious, ready – you could've put a thousand different captions with the picture and they all would've made sense. I just remembered that, just thought of it, for some reason. The different look people can have, at the approach of a highly expected event. "The Highly Expected Event." *(Very brief pause.)* But the point, possibly, is that there are many more right ways to be than wrong ways. Or, that we're all eventually going to do the exact same thing, but, in our own way.

Brief pause.

You know who would've loved all this, by the way? *(A small gesture.)* I am aware that I just said "all this" and made a little gesture towards,

17

you know, this. *(Referring to a couple cardboard boxes, nothing very impressive.)* But, seriously, you know who would've loved it? You know who would've loved being here? On Earth? Alive?

Brief pause. A small perhaps rueful smile. Small trouble with swallowing.

The train was… so many books I read when I was a kid had trains in them. And, the trains…

Pause. Very slight shake of his head, "no." He is having some trouble, and will take a moment. All very underplayed so that we really don't know what's happening. Is he in control? Is this just a very long pause? Did he forget what he wanted to say?

Sorry.

(Quietly.) I could go for something cold. Some lemon sherbet. Not important. In case you wondered, that was not important. Onward. No rest for the whatever-I-am.

Very brief pause. He looks at his index cards.

(To himself.) Oh, that's right. *(To AUDIENCE.)* I thought we might try something. It's similar to the gratitude thing, but there's no sound that goes with it. All it is is, you picture a human being. Anyone you like, real or not, living or dead, and you just really picture them. What are they wearing? Is it daytime or night? Are they holding anything? You can close your

eyes if you want. This is hard to do, but take a breath, ask your brain to be patient with you. Actually, you should definitely close your eyes. Back to your person. Where are they? Are they indoors, or out?

He clicks the remote. PROJECTION and SOUND DESIGN below begin around here.

Do they look like they need anything? Are you even doing this? Try to look into their eyes. Are they older or younger than they should be? Are they about to say something?

PROJECTION: *Slow and gentle rise of a yellow and, eventually, almost blindingly bright sun on desert sands, supported with lights that aim into the audience, and sound design.*

GUY: Don't worry about that. It's just the sun, a picture of the sun. Are you still hanging on to your person? Did they react? Did they turn toward you, away from the light? For some people, the light makes the body disappear, but hopefully you still have the feeling of the person. The spirit. *(As if to a person who's standing.)* Yeah, that's totally all right, if you want to stand up. Are you still together? Sometimes they smile.

PROJECTION: *Slowly changes to a different image. Perhaps a dock on a quiet lake, under a star-filled night, e.g., or something cool and blue, with appropriate sound design, such as a very subtle sound of waves lapping at the shore. Lights on audience should switch to cooler blue color, also very subtly.*

GUY: Okay. Now, they're here. Your special person, living or dead. All quiet, as the stars begin to twinkle. The long day is over. *(Very brief pause.)* You can tuck them in and say good night, anything that feels right, including nothing. Sometimes, I like to hold hands for a while. While the image slowly dissolves in the head.

(Brief pause.) And… whhhssshhhhhh. *(He makes the sound of a mental image gently blowing away.)*

GUY: Nice. *(Very brief pause. Gently and quietly.)* That's supposed to help you sleep, they say. And, actually, they say it can help you stay awake, too. So, good for a lot of things. Being able to picture someone else and just carry your picture through the day. And who knows what amazing things it might do for the person you're picturing. Give whoever it was a call, if they're real or still living.

Brief pause.

Maybe we can take a second and just share a little moment of –

SOUND: *He's interrupted by a song playing, seemingly a ring-tone from a phone, at a VERY low volume.*

"Raindrops Keep Falling on My Head," in a
MUZAC version, or another old Easy-Listening hit.
Maybe the speakers are under the floor or somehow
very difficult to locate?

GUY: What is that – is that a phone?

It only plays for a few seconds and then disappears.

(Brief pause.) "Raindrops Keep Falling on My
Head." *(Or the title of the song, or a line from it,*
if a different one is used.)

Sorry about all these – I mean, they're not
interruptions. They're things, and they're fine.

SOUND: *Sound of "you have a new voicemail" alert. To*
which GUY responds in a very small real way. A
small gesture as if to say, "of course."

GUY: You know what else is great, by the way? Solid
food. A Saltine. A sardine. We probably take
almost everything in existence for granted. A
million miracles at work in this room, right
now, easily. You can almost hear them. Wowee.
Your body produced 5 million red blood cells
in the time since I said "Wowee." You will
produce two swimming pools' worth of saliva
in your life. *(Very brief pause.)* Use it wisely.

He looks at another index card. He reads:

"Figs are rich in iron." Don't know why
I wrote that one. It's true, I guess and we're

21

here seeking the truth. So, there you go: Figs, lot of iron. I delivered. And so now, in return, what are you going to do? Here in the second part of your life? With your hopefully slightly differently shaped Anterior Cingulate Cortex, or ACC, in case we mention it again? What are you going to do?

SOUND: *A "chirp" from a smoke alarm with a dying battery.*

GUY: You have to love this, by the way. You don't have to. But, even if you dislike this particular event, you have to appreciate the larger terms that allow it to exist. The conventions and traditions and understandings passed down through the ages, through grandmothers and school kids and famous Europeans. I know it's hardly the rage anymore, to go out with actual people to an actual place. But, here we are, and, where else? Honestly, where else can a person have that particular in-your-body out-of-body experience? That thing where you're going a mile a minute and sitting quietly in a chair. The levels, you know? *(Has a little trouble getting through the next two words.)* The levels.

(Quietly clears throat and gingerly tries to swallow.)
Excuse me, one second.

He slowly takes out a small juice box and begins to put the small attached straw into it.

SOUND and PROJECTION: *Behind and around him: there is a slowly rising sound of pounding horse hooves and, after a few seconds, a projection of a cave painting of a horse comes up on the wall, slowly scaling in. Then a video of kids riding bikes in the rain, or playing quietly, with some unthreatening thunder in the background, then an image of a lush green Celtic burial mound with audio of mournful bagpipes playing, just as GUY begins to take a sip. It might look for a moment like he's playing a tiny little instrument. Video and sound end. GUY hardly pays any attention. He swallows another small sip, and it seems painful.*

GUY: There. That's good. I'm sorry I don't have enough for everyone. *(Brief pause. Referring to the video and sound, having played for about a minute, in total.)* I don't know what all that was. Horsies.

Brief pause.

I'm sorry if I'm… I'm not usually so disorganized.

He is trying to describe how he feels in this exact moment:

Imagine packing for a trip, and you don't know where or what weather or for how long or why you're going in the first place. Or, I don't know, how about this: the important thing isn't what's gone or lost, it's seeing and knowing what's still there and how it can grow.

Brief pause.

23

SOUND: *crickets; that is, actual sound of crickets.*

GUY: *(Slightly annoyed, though very mildly amused. To BOOTH.)* Is that crickets? That's very funny. *(To BOOTH, amiably.)* I'm glad you're having fun. *(To AUDIENCE.)* Sorry, if this is, I don't know. It's a lot of different feelings, and,....

SOUND: *A drum roll, played on a Kettle Drum, begins to play.*

GUY: No. Hey. Stop. *(Sound stops. A little upset.)* Sorry about that. *(Pause.)* Was someone talking about trains?

> *He sits with us, in a sort of unknowable way. We are not sure where he is, what he is thinking, if anything.*

Where did you go? Everybody seemed like they were a million miles away. *(Brief pause.)* Was that you or me?

> *Pause. GUY looks at an index card, puts it aside and it accidentally falls to the floor beside him. He looks at another, which he also lets fall to the floor. LISA, from off-stage, sort of muffled:*

LISA: Hello?

SOUND: *some very subtle birdsong. accompanies LISA's entrance, It fades gently.*

> *GUY shows in the smallest ways that he is not sure what is going on. He mainly seems to be waiting, in a neutral*

way, for more information, so that he can know what is happening.

LISA: *(Enters, carrying a dining room chair.)* Hi. Am I early?

GUY: Is this about this? Sorry.

LISA: No, no, everything's okay. I don't know if you remember me. Lisa? I'm just here to help out a little. I brought a chair.

LISA puts her chair down, and places her purse/bag, a small cooler to keep things cold, and a Thermos, somewhere nearby.

GUY: I thought you were a friend of Chris and Michelle's.

LISA: Nope. Who are Chris and Michelle?

She waits for an answer. It seems he didn't hear the question. LISA sits down near GUY. Referring to his index cards:

LISA: Are you studying for a test?

GUY nods, a small smile. A pause. He is waiting for her to talk. She is content to sit quietly.

GUY: Well, welcome. Good to have you.

LISA: No, I'm happy to be here. *(Very brief pause.)* Do you remember me?

GUY: A little.

LISA: It's okay if you forgot.

GUY: There's been a lot of people.

LISA: No, of course.

GUY: So, you'll be… *(Said sort of to* AUDIENCE, *hoping that she'll let us all know what she'll be doing.)*

LISA: I'm really just here to be here. And, of course, let me know if there's anything I can do.

GUY: Thanks, thank you. I will.

LISA: Some people like to talk, some people don't. Just be yourself. That's what most people do. That's what everyone does, I guess. *(She takes a phone out of her bag and checks the time and sets it down on a box she has set up like a small table.)*

Brief pause.

SOUND: *another "chirp" from the smoke alarm. To* AUDIENCE, *still calmly and easily, but maybe a little fuzzily:*

GUY: Um. So, what were we, what was the topic? *(Very brief pause.)* There were a couple tockips. Topics.

LISA smiles and takes out her Thermos or sports bottle. She drinks a sip.

LISA: *(Sounding out the word.)* Hibiscus. *(GUY turns to look at her.)* Do you want some?

GUY: No, thanks.

LISA: *(As she looks through her bag.)* I forgot my notebook. *(Pulls out a little bottle of toy bubbles, sets it somewhere. Very small self-deprecating laugh.)* But I remembered this. My kids are crazy about bubbles. My father-in-law, too.

GUY: Yeah, I like bubbles, too.

LISA: We can do some later. If you want. They're silly. I'll be right back. *(She exits.)*

GUY: Never a dull moment. *(A long dull pause. He stares at the audience without moving much.)* Maybe not *never.*

Brief pause.

It's… so – you've been great, first of all. But, so, there's the plan, some idea, and then there's nature, and you, everyone, you adjust. And your life, is the adjustment. To the real things. So, you have to love the plan, and, love the adjustment, in yourself, and, everywhere. Am I talking too loud? I don't mean "too loud." Ten seconds. I just need a little ten seconds. *(It's best if he DOES NOT talk any louder, as or before he's saying "…talking too loud." Just normal volume, all around.)*

27

He sits with us for ten seconds or so. Looking at us but maybe a million miles away. And then:

I haven't forgotten about you.

He looks, with a little effort, at his index cards.

These are, this'll be fun.

He clicks the remote and on the wall appears a movie-preview-style JUMBLE QUIZ.

PROJECTION: *"CITY OF LIGHTS?" "SPIAR" (After some time, the letters re-arrange themselves into "PARIS.")*

GUY: Paris. Paris, France. *(He clicks remote.)*

PROJECTION: *"SITE OF THE 1912 OLYMPICS?" "CHOMSKOLT"*

LISA: *(Enters, with her notebook. As she looks up at the projection:)* Oh, wow – the Olympics were in Chomskolt?

GUY: No. Watch.

PROJECTION: *The letters "CHOMSTOLK" re-arrange themselves into "ANSWER." GUY clicks off the screen.*

LISA: I thought it was going to be Stockholm. *(She picks up some index cards that GUY dropped earlier.)*

GUY: I guess someone was having fun with these.

LISA: *(She reads from one of the cards.)* "My birth is–"
Sorry. Can I read this?

GUY: *(Not entirely comfortable with her reading his
cards.)* Sure.

LISA: "My birth is imminent. Forgive me, brethren,
sistren. But do not prevent me from coming to
life." What's that from?

GUY: *(Taking it back from her and looking at it.)* Is it – I
don't know. I wrote it down.

LISA: I love quotes.

GUY: Yeah.

LISA: *(Brief pause.)* "A dog knows it's not a cat and
a giraffe knows it's a giraffe. But you braying
squealing asses do not know you are asses."
(Very brief pause.) That was a needlepoint my
mom had. I forget who said it. *(She sits back
down.)* Are you sure you don't want some?
(Offering tea.)

GUY: No, thanks. I don't think I can…. *(Very small
sound of frustration.)* Uhh. I'm sorry I'm so
disorganized.

LISA: We're all exactly as organized as we need to
be. Do you want a pillow or anything?

GUY: I had notes, these cards. The little colored tabs. I had a whole plan.

LISA: But that changed?

GUY: Yeah.

LISA: That's hard. And so now you're adapting?

GUY: Yeah. That's a good word. Yes. It's two things. There's the old idea to let go of and the new one to get used to. The new thing keeps changing and the old thing keeps getting farther away. *(To LISA, as she moves toward him.)* And I'm trying to… I just wish…

LISA: Let me know if this is all right. *(She puts a cold washcloth on his forehead.)* This was my mom's go-to thing. *(She stands behind him as he puts his hand to the towel to hold it to his head.)*

GUY: I wish I could sleep.

LISA: You can sleep. *(She rests her hands lightly on his shoulders.)*

GUY: I felt like I was really starting to get somewhere.

LISA: You were.

GUY: And everybody's so nice. I know I'm letting people down.

LISA: No, you're not. We're fine. We'll think of something. You just try and relax.

GUY: Okay. *(He closes his eyes.)*

A brief pause.

LISA, standing a few feet behind GUY, makes a gesture with her hands around him, as if she is surrounding him with a protective aura. Then she takes a step or two, maybe stretches her calf. She then does a short dance piece, using simple, common movements. There is no music and it seems to be almost ceremonial, as if she is blessing him, or interceding on his behalf with some heavenly being. She finishes her dance, maybe a very little bow toward upstage. She then quietly and unfussily sits down, looking at us for a moment, as she does. She checks in on GUY, who is still sleeping, and makes a note in her notebook. She has a sip of tea.

LISA: *(Quietly, to AUDIENCE.)* I forget to move around, so I started doing a little dance as part of my day. It helps make things more, just, it keeps things moving. *(Brief pause.)* Sometimes I take a class. I know nobody asked. *(Brief pause.)* I just want you to understand everything. As much as I can help you with, which is, you know, that's limited. *(She checks time on her phone.)* It's 8:46 *(Or whatever the actual time is.)*

She writes another note in her notebook. GUY opens his eyes.

(Gently.) There he is.

31

GUY: *(Taking the towel off his head.)* What is this?

LISA: Was that nice? A little nap?

GUY: Um, thanks, yes.

A little shyly, to AUDIENCE:

What's… how's everyone doing?

LISA: *(She waits to see if anyone else will answer.)* All good. No news.

GUY: How long did I sleep? What time is it?

LISA: 10:47. *(Brief pause.)* Sorry, no, 8:47. 8:48.

GUY: Wow. *(To the audience.)* I'm sorry. That probably wasn't very entertaining.

LISA: Well, luckily there's a whole world. Oh, I almost forgot. Excuse me. *(She exits.)*

GUY sits for a moment, then gets up, spilling some cards that were tucked under him onto the floor, and walks a little uneasily downstage. Brief pause. He looks out and up toward the booth or the heavens.

GUY: Is it – *(Much louder.)* Is it now!?

LISA: *(Pause. From off-stage.)* Were you saying something?

GUY: Yeah. I was yelling.

LISA: *(As she enters, carrying a small paper bag.)* Are you okay?

GUY: *(Very quietly.)* Mm-hmm. *(He sits back down in his wheelchair. She takes a card from his hand and the remote control clicker. She helps him get settled.)*

LISA: Here. *(She hands him the bag.)*

GUY: *(He looks inside.)* What are these? Oh, fortune cookies. *(Flatly.)* Fun. *(He rests the bag on his thigh.)*

LISA: Do you want to read one? See what it says? *(He doesn't really respond. LISA gently takes the bag and sets it down.)* Do you want to do another one of those word jumbles?

GUY: Yeah.

SOUND and LIGHT: *She clicks the remote and loud rock music and bright lighting come on, maybe a few seconds of the song that will play at the end. She manages to quickly turn it off, within a second or two. She hands the remote to him.*

LISA: Here.

GUY: Yeah, that's... *(Happy to have a little problem he can solve. "How the remote control works." Referring to the technology, a basic little statement.)* All this stuff is connected. *(He clicks it.)*

PROJECTION: *JUMBLE QUIZ. It's the ALPHABET, which then scrambles itself into the SANSKRIT ALPHABET.*

(He looks at this for a little while. Very quietly.)
Hmm.

LISA: *(Pause.)* I did your guided exercise, earlier. Picturing someone? I was waiting in the hallway and listening.

GUY: Oh.

LISA: I pictured my uncle Albert.

GUY: Oh, good. Was it good?

LISA: Yeah. It was. *(Brief pause.)* In my own experience, I… I haven't talked to people who are gone. I know that people do and I've heard so many stories, of course. But just not in my experience.

GUY: No. I didn't mean to – maybe it's different for different people.

LISA: Well, yes, exactly. Because I really saw Albert. And, and this was fun, we talked. In a really regular way. He said I should go to Iceland, this summer. He said it's okay if I get impatient but I should try not to. I could hear him and feel his voice, kind of.

GUY: That sounds like a good conversation.

LISA: Yeah. It was. I wasn't really trying. You just have to kind of let go, I guess. It's, also, he was just really clear when he was alive, you knew where he stood on things.

GUY: Yeah.

LISA: And so he still seems really clear. That seems like a life lesson.

GUY: Life lessons are great. *(Brief pause. "That's not very interesting." To AUDIENCE, simply and humbly.)* That would probably sound pretty good in Latin.

LISA: That whole thing about the afterlife or not, as if there's one big final answer – I'm sorry, I don't mean to suddenly–

GUY: No, go ahead.

LISA: It just suddenly seemed really simple. Albert died a while ago, but we talked just now – in my head, yes, but – we talked, and so he's not gone, he's here, and he'll never be gone as long as – well, maybe he'll be gone when I'm gone and all the other people who talk with him are gone, but by then, maybe someone is going to be talking with me. Maybe someone'll need me to still be here and so there'll be this whole long line of loving whispering people, down through the ages.

GUY: Yes.

LISA: *(Adjusting the cuff of her pants or scratching her shin.)* It felt good. Talking and knowing someone loved you, that they love you still. Or hearing them. It makes the world seem smaller. That was all sort of a jumble. *(Very brief pause.)* Like the word things.

GUY: No. I think I followed.

LISA: *(Brief pause.)* My uncle told me "Pack, and Unpack." What do you think that means?

GUY: I don't know but I like it. Pack and unpack. *(He mouths the words.)*

LISA: *(Brief pause.)* You probably have a lot on your mind.

GUY: I'm so angry.

LISA: You're angry?

GUY: No. I meant the other one.

LISA: Another word? *(He doesn't respond.)* Do you want some more cold water?

GUY: I don't think…

LISA: For your forehead?

GUY: No. *(Pause. Simply, quietly.)* It's in a big field. A tent in a big meadow. There's music and all my favorite foods. And I want to go over, but they're checking people's wristbands and I want to know if I can bring plates of food back out for everyone. For my family and everyone.

LISA: Was this a dream?

GUY: No.

LISA: You wanted to share with everyone and make sure they were all okay.

GUY: Yeah. Like anyone would.

LISA: But this is you.

GUY: This is me.

LISA: And they're, what?, calling numbers? Like, tickets?

GUY: And I know I'm being called in. Wristbands with a number between 400 and 600. *(He fusses with his slipper for a moment.)* And I'm worried about everyone.

LISA: *(She moves her chair closer. She whispers something, and then gently takes his slippers off. She gets back to her chair.)* I heard such nice things from people. From some of the parents of the kids that you – what did you do, you coached swimming?

GUY: Swimming and diving. Can you believe it? That I used to do that?

LISA: They said you really gave them things they
could use. Courage and all that, but also good,
regular things, like paper plates of food.

GUY: They probably give me too much credit.

LISA: Do you want to try to picture everyone? At the
– what was it, like, a picnic?

GUY: Picnic. Music festival.

LISA: Can you see them? What are they doing?

*Brief pause. He's seeing the scene in some deep faraway
way. Maybe some tears trying to come, but there is also
something restrained and very clear about the way he
speaks. This is a different scene for him, now. The world
is letting him go.*

GUY: I think they want me to go in, to go through.
To go listen to the music. They want me to eat
whatever I want. There's another area across
the road where you don't need a wristband.
And they have stuff there for everyone. Food
and free T-shirts.

LISA: So they'll be okay?

GUY: Yeah. I hope so. *(Brief pause.)* What should I do
now?

LISA: You don't have to do anything.

GUY: But I want to.

LISA: Do you want to read one of your cards?

GUY: Okay. *(Reads.)* "Can there be a – ." Some were just notes or questions.

LISA: I love notes or questions.

GUY: *(He reads.)* "Can there be a smoke machine?"

LISA: That sounds fun. What's that for? *(Brief pause.)* Do you want to read another?

GUY: *(He looks through two or three cards to see if there's something worth sharing.)* No, I'm all right.

LISA: What would you   GUY: I'm hoping we
       like to–   can–

LISA: Go ahead.

GUY: *(He clears his throat, swallows.)* Last Words are – *(Swallows.)* Last Words are something everyone talks about and writes books. But I hope we can… *(Clears throat again.)* Sorry. I was hoping we could think about First Words. "Doggie." "Bopple." *(The following two words are said just the TINIEST bit as if he is calling out for them.)* "Mommy, Daddy." "Wabbit." I love when little kids talk. "Skelekin." "Choo-choo." It's amazing. The things we can share. The world, the worlds. *(Very brief pause. With sadness but some good-natured ease.)* I thought I had more time. *(Brief pause.)* I'm sorry. I'm not here anymore.

LISA: *(Gently.)* Where are you?

GUY: *(Said as if he's still in the exact same place.)* I'm
       here.

       *The following is very quiet. Even LISA who is sitting close
       to him, cannot hear him:*

       (Inaudible.) I just wanted to say a few more
       things.

LISA: Sorry?

       *She leans closer and he speaks, in a very faint whisper.
       She leans very close to him, listens to his whisper, and then
       repeats what he says to the audience.*

       "It's been so nice being here with you all."

       (Again, as above.) "I'll never forget it."

       He whispers, and she can't understand.

       Sorry? I didn't…

       *She leans in and he whispers again. She whispers to GUY
       to be sure she's understood him correctly.*

       (To AUDIENCE, with the accompanying gesture.)
       "Thumbs up."

       *He smiles, shakes his head almost imperceptibly. LISA sits
       back a little in her chair, looks out at us, looks around at
       the different faces, all very easy and gentle movements,*

nothing too precious. GUY's small shake of his head, as in saying "no," increases and changes, in the tiniest way, so that perhaps he is making tiny circles with his head, instead of going side to side. Again, these are the slightest gestures. He mouths a word or two, almost imperceptibly. He gets still. He takes in the room, with only his eyes. Very quietly, but in a regular voice with a simple delivery, NOT as a big message, but more as a simple parting thought.)

GUY: Take care of each other.

LISA: *(Brief pause. Gently, to AUDIENCE.)* Did you hear that?

GUY looks at us for a while. He is very close to the end. He seems scared but also exhausted and resolved. He is very still. Perhaps his breath, almost inaudible, quickens a bit. The tiniest of moments. He closes his eyes and lowers his head, as if he's fallen asleep. His hands are resting on his thighs.

SOUND: *A single "chirp" from the smoke alarm.*

LISA touches his arm. She gently rolls up his cuff and checks his pulse. She looks to the audience and smiles a small, sad, but loving smile, while she's checking. GUY has died. She rolls his cuff back down. She then stands and makes a note in her notebook, checking the time. She takes care of some other details, very gently, very quietly. She picks up the bag of fortune cookies, glances around for a trash can, and then comes to the front of the stage and hands one to an audience member. She leaves the bag on the front of the stage, and gestures in the smallest of ways to let us know that she's leaving them there for us. She begins to

wheel GUY off the stage. She stops when his back is to us.
She uses his clicker to put on some music for us. Her first
click brings up a gentle light on the doorway. She clicks
again and the light goes down slightly. The doorway is at
her back, so she doesn't notice the lights going up or down,
as she is concentrating on getting some music or video to
play. She clicks again and some version of the ghost music
at the top of the show comes on, though it's a tiny bit more
like music. We also see the rectangle of a video projection,
though there is no projection yet. LISA gently wheels GUY
off-stage. This moment, with video gray and semi-music,
continues for a little while.

A simple but mesmerizing video projection begins.
Perhaps a nature show or something that is easy to watch
and doesn't feel as if it's making great claims about the
final meaning of the play. The premiere production used
documentary footage of penguins, slightly slowed down.
The video slowly evolves and a song begins (in the premiere
this was "Love Athena," by Olivia Tremor Control). Song
and video images gently begin to go together, and perhaps
increase in volume and to a constant and quick-cutting
flow. Ultimately, as much life and color and energy and
humanness and diversity and joy should come into the
theatre, via the video. Older people dancing, a child bearing
a corner of a coffin, newlyweds, children on a playground,
all of it. Throughout the roughly two and half minutes of
the song, a riotous and joyous scene should break out. Bright
flashing lights on the audience. A bubble machine sending
bubbles floating down into the crowd. A haze machine.
Glorious disco-ball lighting, perhaps from a mirror-ball
that has been revealed on the stage, so that it is close to
eye-level. All timed to build and grow with the music.
It really should be an incredible rock and roll show, but

one that has built organically and even gently. Toward the very end of the song, balloons drop from the ceiling. Volunteers – with the music, lights, and video still going – quickly and unobtrusively place baskets on the stage and near the exits that contain fortune cookies, juice boxes, party favors like stress balls and little plastic wrist bands, and t-shirts. Small signs on the baskets will say "Please Help Yourselves." (Contact the author's representation for the particular messages of the fortune cookies, wrist bands, or any other details of this part.) The calendar drops off the wall. With the final sounds of the song, everything crashes to a stop, and then it's dark and quiet. A pause in the dark, five seconds or so, and then lights gently rise.

A simple curtain call.

In the lobby outside the theatre, there will be coffee cake on paper plates and cups of punch. Some figs and lollipops. Ideally, this little part would serve as a second act, in which people talk and say hi and stand around for a moment. Some signs, in the same font as the basket signs, will say "This is for you." And, "Figs." Etc. Music should be playing, in the lobby. Anything that encourages people to linger for a moment.

END

SOME ADDITIONAL PRODUCTION NOTES:

PROPS: *wheelchair, with a small bell mounted on it; some pockets on the wheelchair in which there is: a sandwich; a juice box; and, some index cards with notes written on them, wrapped in a rubber band. A remote "clicker" device, placed somewhere among some boxes. Seven to ten nice pens should be placed on the floor, here and there, among the rows of seats. They should be spaced so that no one person who finds a pen would likely see another person finding one.*

GENERAL NOTE: *Production elements and design should probably tend more toward the elegantly invisible than toward the slick. That is, perhaps things that are quietly surprising and magical, but that are subtle and sly enough that they might end up being more felt than consciously seen. As an example, a sound effect of truck brakes squealing, outside the theatre, and down the street, and other things from the "world outside," regular sounds that might have an eerie or mournful or beautiful feel inside the theater. All of course to be used sparingly and at close to subliminal levels. But, of course, the celebration at the end should be as vibrant, intense, colorful, and gorgeously organized as possible.*

A THOUGHT ON PERFORMANCE AND DIRECTION: *The general approach should be simple, grounded, and incredibly specific without being fussy. GUY's illness should mainly be seen through cracks and momentary lapses. If hospice is a model, for the latter part of the play, then we should know that sometimes, in hospice, people get grouchy, bored, energized, and that they have moments of absolute and unsentimental clarity about what is happening. There can be a matter-of-factness to things. This is not a play about aging. The normal clichés and stereotypes of the aging process would probably obscure the message and could seem sentimental. This is, however, partly a play about dying, most likely from cancer, so that the process is more of a sometimes gentle but steady leaving of energy and spirit and voice, despite one's best hopes and efforts, rather than a heavily-acted aging and slowing-down process. Although, all that said, every effort should be made to perform GUY's journey in as detailed and specific and clear way as possible. For example, GUY might fuss with his slipper, showing us that he feels some discomfort or pain in his foot, on page 27, on the line "We probably take almost everything in existence for granted." He will fuss with the slipper again on page 43, as his foot is still bothering him, and LISA will remove his slippers. Every opportunity should be taken to create a real, at times almost invisible, through-line like this. GUY's disappearance from us should be gradual, incredibly subtle, and real.*

Lastly, and maybe most importantly, I hope that the experience of the play, for the audience, has mostly do to with living, living well, living with gratitude and openness and joy, and I hope and believe that that sense and feeling of the play is best served, in both performance and production, with simplicity and specificity.

WILL ENO lives in Brooklyn with his wife Maria Dizzia and their daughter Albertine. He is a Residency Five Fellow of the Signature Theatre in New York. His 2004 Pulitzer-finalist play, *Thom Pain (based on nothing)*, was presented there in 2018, in a heralded and sold-out revival starring Michael C. Hall and directed by Oliver Butler. Signature also produced and premiered *Title and Deed* in 2012, *The Open House* in 2014, and *Wakey, Wakey* in 2017. Following an acclaimed run at Yale Repertory Theatre, his play *The Realistic Joneses* appeared on Broadway in 2014, where it won a Drama Desk Award, was named *USA Today*'s "Best Play on Broadway," topped the *Guardian*'s 2014 list of American plays, and was included in the *New York Times*' "Best Theatre of 2014." *The Open House* won the 2014 Obie Award, the Lortel Award for Outstanding Play, and a Drama Desk Award, and was included in both the *Time Out New York* and *Time* magazine Top 10 Plays of the Year. The lauded London premiere was directed by Sir Michael Boyd at The Print Room. Will's play *Gnit*, an adaptation of *Peer Gynt*, premiered at the Actors Theatre of Louisville in 2013. *Title and Deed* was on the *New York Times* and the *New Yorker* magazine's Top Ten Plays of 2012. *Middletown*, winner of the Horton Foote Prize, premiered at the Vineyard Theatre and subsequently at Steppenwolf Theatre and many other American theaters and universities. The Canadian premiere, at The Shaw Festival in 2017, received a rapturous response from critics and audiences and was remounted in 2018 at Crow's Theatre in Toronto. *Thom Pain (based on nothing)* ran at the Geffen Playhouse in 2016 and starred Rainn Wilson; this production served as the basis for a film version directed by Oliver Butler and Will, which premiered at the Memphis Film Festival and is available to stream on BroadwayHD. The play has been translated into more than a dozen languages. He was recently awarded the PEN/Laura Pels International Foundation Award. His plays are published by Samuel French, TCG, Dramatists Play Service, Playscripts, and Oberon Books.